Community Learning & Libraries
Cymuned Ddysgu a Llyfrgelloedd

This item should be returned or renewed by the last date stamped below.

To renew telephone: 656656 or 656657 (minicom) or www.newport.gov.uk/libraries

ENRICHING LEARNING IN NEWPORT SCHOOLS

ELIN	
Z780706	
PETERS	29-Oct-2012
577.7	£9.99

LIVING AND NON-LIVING

Ocean

Cassie Mayer

www.heinemann.co.uk/library

Visit our website to find out more information about Heinemann Library books.

To order:

☎ Phone 44 (0) 1865 888066

▤ Send a fax to 44 (0) 1865 314091

▢ Visit the Heinemann Bookshop at www.heinemann.co.uk/library to browse our catalogue and order online.

First published in Great Britain by Heinemann Library,
Halley Court, Jordan Hill, Oxford OX2 8EJ, part of Pearson Education.
Heinemann is a registered trademark of Pearson Education Ltd.

Editorial: Cassie Mayer and Diyan Leake
Design: Kimberly Miracle
Illustration: Mark Beech
Picture research: Erica Martin and Melissa Allison
Production: Duncan Gilbert

Origination by Modern Age
Printed and bound in China by South China
Printing Co. Ltd

ISBN 978 0 431 18463 0 (hardback)
12 11 10 09
10 9 8 7 6 5 4 3 2

ISBN 978 0 431 18468 5 (paperbackback)
12 11 10 09 08
10 9 8 7 6 5 4 3 2 1

British Library Cataloguing in Publication Data
Mayer, Cassie
  Living and Non-living: Ocean

A full catalogue record for this book is available from the British Library.

Acknowledgements
The publishers would like to thank the following for permission to reproduce photographs: Alamy pp. **7** (Adam Butler), **8** (Reinhard Dirscherl), **9** (Andre Seale); Corbis pp. **18** (Jim Richardson), **21** (Stephen Frink), **back cover** (Jim Richardson); FLPA pp. **14** (Ariadne Van Zandbergen); Getty Images p. **6** (Jeff Hunter); NHPA p. **10** (Michael Patrick O'Neill); Nature Picture Library pp. **5** (Constantinos Petrinos), **11** (Brandon Cole), **13** (Georgette Douwma), **17** (Jose B. Ruiz), **19** (Jurgen Freund), **20** (Doug Wechsler), **22** (Francis Abbott), **23** (habitat image: Constantinos Petrinos; kelp: Brandon Cole); Photolibrary pp. **4** (Tobias Bernhard), **12** (Karen Gowlett-Holmes), **15** (Pacific Stock), **16** (Animals Animals/Earth Scene), **23** (ocean image: Tobias Bernhard).

Cover photograph of a coral reef in the Red Sea reproduced with permission of Nature Picture Library (Georgette Douwma).

Every effort has been made to contact copyright holders of any material reproduces in this book. Any omissions will be rectified in subsequent printings if notice is given to the publisher.

Contents

An ocean habitat

An ocean is an area of water.
An ocean is very big.

An ocean has living things.
An ocean has non-living things.

Fish

parrotfish

Is a fish a living thing?

Does a fish need food? *Yes.*
Does a fish need water? *Yes.*

Does a fish need air? *Yes.*

Does a fish grow? *Yes.*

So a fish is a living thing.

Seaweed

Is seaweed a living thing?

Sunshine makes plant food.

Does seaweed need food? *Yes.*
Does seaweed need water? *Yes.*

Does seaweed need air? *Yes.*

Does seaweed grow? *Yes.*

So seaweed is a living thing.

Sand

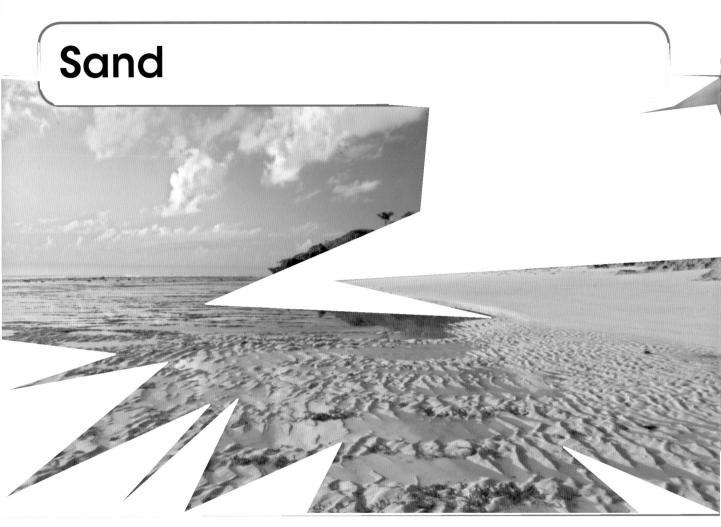

Is sand a living thing?

Does sand need food? *No*.
Does sand need water? *No*.

Does sand need air? *No*.

Does sand grow? *No*.

So sand is not a living thing.

Starfish

Is a starfish a living thing?

clam

Does a starfish need food? *Yes.*
Does a starfish need water? *Yes.*

Does a starfish need air? *Yes.*

Does a starfish grow? *Yes.*

So a starfish is a living thing.

An ocean is home to many things.
An ocean is an important habitat.

Picture glossary

 **habitat** area where plants and animals live

 **ocean** very large area of salty water

 **seaweed** plant that grows in water

Index

Notes for parents and teachers
Before reading
Talk to the children about living and non-living things. Show them a picture of a fish and a rock. Which is living? How do they know?
After reading
Create an underwater picture. Dampen a large piece of paper and while the paper is still wet, paint shades of blue and green. Allow the colours to merge. Make fish by painting handprints on scraps of coloured card or paper. Cut out and turn sideways. Add a goggle eye and a mouth. Stick the fish in shoals on the paper. When the paper is dry, cut strips of clear, blue and green Cellophane and stick lengths to the paper to give a watery effect.
Read *The Rainbow Fish* by Marcus Pfister.